Your Eureka Not Mined

Your Eureka Not Mined

Poems

Christopher T. Keaveney

Broadstone Books

Library of Congress Control Number 2016962418

ISBN 978-1-937968-31-1

Cover and Interior Design by Laurie Powers

Broadstone Books
An Imprint of
Broadstone Media LLC
418 Ann Street
Frankfort, KY 40601-1929
BroadstoneBooks.com

For Shigeko

CONTENTS

III. White Knuckled in My Adoration 47

IV. Mind Your Eureka 63

I. INTIMATES OF LIGHT

IN THE ATTIC OF SMALL REMEMBRANCES

She reimagined the city of her birth
as a form of resignation,
as a series of concentric circles
widening in lazy arcs
from an uncertain source,
a plunk whose volume
increased with each hearing.
This made the brownstone
stillness of her adopted home
easier to bear,
a calcification of refusals
and sleights that she rocked
into submission each night
like a colicky infant.

Surface to air,
the low-slung orbit
of the nuthatch
in the backyard of long gone neighbors
proved both premonition
and sustenance
during her infrequent visits home.
The wheezing of the floorboards
in the dusty bedroom
she had shared with her younger sister
riffed on an uncle's accordion bluster
that had been the sisters'
inside joke.

On the night her mother died
she found herself feigning sleep
in the room
where the woman had sighed away
forty years of solitude,
an absent husband reduced
to the slicing of moonlight
through the blinds,
to the scuttle of mice
in walls that clung hard
to nicotine and unfulfilled promises.

Squatter's rights,
the didgeridoo rattle
of a smoker's hack
in those final years,
the way the creation myth
her mother had shared with her
as a child
always started
with a patient woman
and ended with despair,
a plea she had come
to recognize
as the trepanning of tedium,
as the harried beating of wings
that had come to mistrust gravity.

AN UNHURRIED LUMINESCENCE

The girl in the cape
keeps returning to the spot
where her father should have been waiting,
a simple promise made
over cheesecake.

The buckle in the cobblestones
in the far reaches of the park
reveals a different story,
a parsing of sunlight on broken glass
to underscore
the pulsing adoration of the bodega.

Smack dab where
he left you
prey to
the preposterous dimensions
of premonition.

I won't be long.

There was no note,
just a recovery
from the river
on a cold November morning.
Unfettered truths,
the gasp of recognition
before the sheet was raised
one final time.

Held aloft,
the shimmer of a found coin
reckons
an epiphany
irreducible in a child's clasp,
the flash coming as afterthought,
a promise made and meant
but not kept.

BOY WONDER

Cartwheeling
toward serenity
through a waft of bluefish,
early July
in Shinnecock Hills
where children straddle a dirt path,
boys in bow ties
sidling for the sake of sidling,
the girls patient in patent leather.

I would not hold
that against you,
would not wait
in mock adoration
for the men
to unwrap their catch,
slowly,
almost reverently,
the echo of their voices
on Chalk Hill
and Fairy Tale Forest
among the pitch pines,
where a flattening of pennies
on train tracks
shines for an instant
like scales fallen
from a boy's eyes.

BALLAD FOR ONE WHO TENDERS THE BAS RELIEF

Much later we came to realize
it had only happened
because we missed the turnoff
to Coffin Bluff.
Undaunted,
on the college visit circuit
you blamed it on Sibelius,
blushing against the jog
of summer's sweet sixteen,
our journey measured in the hay
scuttling the shoulder.
It was on the second afternoon
in a rest area north of Sacramento
that my second daughter
chose to come out
while I fiddled
with the cup holder.

What a saucer full
of dandelions meant
the day after the tea party
that served as your seventh birthday celebration,
elocution as summer breeze
and the reliquary repainted as bird house
in a cramped corner behind the shed.
That was the summer of tee ball,
the newest coach
learning not to fuss the backhand pick.
The legitimacy of the backstop
in and of itself
made no difference.

Life in the shape of a starfish
on a beach visit,
a fanning out of expectations
refined to the rigor mortis
of unanswered pleas,
the way my daughter's flailing hand
invokes the infield fly rule.
What becomes

the legitimacy of the erstwhile explorer,
pail and shovel in hand,
a summer's entropy
refashioned as a daughter's filial piety
come home to roost.
What the leaves in the bottom of the cup
should have said,
had we but waited for them to settle.

Your eureka not mined.

FROM THE RECENTLY DISCOVERED SONNETS OF DU FU

I worry about Cassiopeia,
about the smoke that rises from the bonfires
and the clinching of kelp against the driftwood.
I fret over the gibbous moon

or at least the memory of it,
and I am positively troubled by
the tang of salt dripping from my hood to my lips.
I harbor resentments about the languor

of high tide and the studious arc of the osprey
on bald peak.
It comes down to trust,
steadying the same moon
you court at home in our bed
a thousand *li* away.

My simply wanting you
to walk this beach with me
will never make it so.

I STAND CORRECTED

The frog intended for you,
melon green and tinged with red and squirming
until just now
in my cupped hands

splintered as tributes will,
plumbing
the inflections of stasis.

The squint of indecision
I saw reflected
in the breakfront glass
may have been meant for me,
fingers to tinker
with the grafting.

A BRIEF HISTORY OF DESERTIFICATION

I had a hunch about zephyrs
that I was reluctant to share,
not precisely a theory
but an unrelenting whisper
from inside the mosquito net.
Four days out of a walled city,
we awakened
from the long, star-ridden night
to the pounding
of imagined waves,
to an ocher ooze
that passed for the horizon.
Through the smoke of the breakfast fires
we couldn't help but note
the badly mangled *feng shui*
of the caravan.

How quickly blisters presaged regret
on the sixth day,
reckless speculations
about the true cost of the oasis,
the scarlet ostentation of the hummingbird
and the luxury that was the blessing
on the lips of a merchant
turned seer.

From Day One the nomads' songbook
had been a heaviness in our throats,
an indulgence that stopped
just short of a curse.
Among the unforgiving orthodoxy
of the dunes
the wineskin remained the last vestige of civilization,
a mirage that never pretended to be the thing itself.

LEMMINGESQUE

Not terribly unlike the ocean
from ebb to peter,
a moment's indecision reduced to a lisp of foam,
diligent but varicose

in early September,
Just off Sandy Hook
where the nuclear plant
turned out to be one boy's deliverance.

As tongue-tied as you want me to be
I arrive again an hour too late
for the bonfire.
All that remains
of the rain
after the others have scattered
is the empathy of the wind,
the hard tack of driftwood

and distortion paraphrased as succor,
though in the end
the sand
grants no quarter.
Soft step on the strand,
the footsteps we follow
preordained,
less march than pilgrimage.

MEDEA AS PORTRAYED BY A YOUNGISH JANIS JOPLIN

The blade glint that stokes
rebellion
is spice to the flower
of a saltier wound.
More-or-less presentable
in braids,
frizzy hair ever marks
the outsider,
espresso for the wants
of an abandoned woman.

The ram's horn on the headboard
casts a smaller shadow
the second time around
as the first frost hints
at the hollow
of discovery,
the fleece I rose
to embrace,
caving to covet.

That was the day the wind
learned to astonish me.

SHARKS

Ear to the floor in Tiki's Pizza Palace
where light fled and left us again to our own devices,
the rain picking up
where the wind

dared stir the muslin shadow of bamboo
on a baby's outstretched hand,
sturgeon-ridged and immaculate
as of all intimates of light.

Rendered beady-eyed and cartilaginous,
a primordial swish
trumps a diver's triumph of light,

the cage to mock
of us men,
and always great shadows
cornered but circling,
circling,
hankering after
the red meat of intuition.

THAT WHICH THE WATER EMBRACES

Li Bai
      naturally
byzantine in disarray,
broods over
the inkblot in the margin
where the moan of the gibbon
gives way to the calibrations
of one man's undoing.

What emerges from mist
      hugging
the reedy shore,
are fragments
of the weaver girl's song,
the apostasy
of a flute tucked
into an official's sleeve.

Left to reckon the price
of improvisation
an old man laughs to himself,
wizened
by the world
and by his weakness for the tinkling of the cups.

Ripples mask
one of the many faces
of rebellion,
moonlight seeping through
the poet's outstretched hands.

YOU'LL REMEMBER MATILDA

Standing close to the flames,
the way we wanted to be remembered
instamatic.
A city neither knew well enough
of gas lights and accretions
the furrow which was memory,
the tuck and jog of the immigrants' quarter.

The grandfather remembered
by his hat
and the voice,
what might have passed for a brogue in a time
less ridden by immigrant guilt,

knuckles a reminder of better times.

The only promises that matter
the old man would say
are the ones we make to ourselves.

THE CRUCIVERBALIST'S FIRST AND LAST CLUES

"Bernice Gordon, a self-described cruciverbalist who over the last
six decades contributed some 150 crossword puzzles to The New
York Times, died on Thursday at her home in Philadelphia. She
was 101."

The New York Times, January 30, 2015

The alternative almost always works better,
as in Master Kong's little black book
12 Across
the single highway that runs into
the desert town where you bought me
my first drink and demonstrated
an amazing capacity for wordiness,
exaggerating the down beat
when I least expected it.

Huck's Big Muddy bromance
24 Down
Shadows lengthening on the runway
where you leaned in to say
what I thought was goodbye,
though the words were lost
in the confusion of a forehead kiss
and taxiing that led
inevitably to

Billy Holiday's go-to cocktail
46 Across
aged 31, bored with Uncle Miltie
and the resignation of the failed tupperware
party, 3 kids on a rainy day and no jigsaws,
I turned to dictionaries and graph paper,
as if grief for Mother on the second anniversary of
her death were less precious

than the birthplace of the butcher boy
38 Down
remarriage
and another doubleheader at the Vet,
cookie cutter stadium so unlike
Shibe Park where Father paraded me every Sunday.

Mike Schmidt left in the on-deck circle,
after the unexpected pick-off move
a costly, rookie gaffe

as startling as the fanciest Greek column
6 Across
on the rare family vacation to the Finger Lakes,
the Greek revival promenade
where you suggested we leave the children to their own devices
in the cabin and took my h&
& said what I knew you wanted to say all along,
"The Girl from Ipanema" and stones for skipping.

Permafrost next of kin
33 Across
pancreatic cancer became your unkeyed square
boxing you in for the last time,
the small consolations of my early
puzzles completed one after the other in the IC unit,
while the only taste of spring I could offer
was a clutch of cherry blossoms thrust in a Gatorade bottle,
another X I would learn to bear

like Murasaki rival's cushion
2 Down
sequestered in my study
with the cats and the occasional
grandchild to graph my progress,
I arrange the dictionaries in the usual way
searching for patterns,
and soon enough it's just me and the cats
and the measure of letters
and their tiny weight.

SECRET HANDSHAKE OF THE MINOR BACHS

We were never completely in on the joke,
Leipzig and rhinestones,
the razzing we learned to bear
at a tender age about our inability
to pose it in the form of a question.
Desultory,
as in the pedals never pushed
the stops reluctantly yanked,
the aberrant echo that rattled the nave
in the plain church
where we cut our teeth.
They don't pay you—
the old man liked to remind us
as a matter of course—
to overthink the divertimento.

As teens we churned butter
and drove recalcitrant geese through the town square,
courting village girls in calico and Belgian lace,
simple diversions
to pass the long summer nights.
The clavichord was my undoing,
as the harpsichord yours,
the chronic smell of linseed
and the silhouette that never rose
above juxtaposition,
constant reminders
of our shortcomings.

Poised to perfection,
we stood shoulder to wig,
the official family portrait
that never materialized,
longing to embrace
the hymn that opened our joint composition—
the wisteria
of self immolation—
another metaphor that simply
tried too hard.

Stuck in the caesura
of summer's doggiest days,
we cling to what remains of harmony,
the nebulae of regrets bunched
in a cluster of sharps.
In the end we may be remembered
only for the unfinished cello suite,
the one they called *taciturn*,
a little something
not nearly as well-tempered
as the color in the cheeks
of the rag pickers
in Weimar's fugue-shaped alleys.

SPRINGTIME IN WATERTOWN

As if Cuneiform were a verb
bracing for discovery,
the compass
and the companion star
fail to agree.

Sometimes the sunshine
resolves itself this way
as paraphrase
of wax paper and delirium,
fumbling for something
just out of reach,

the grain that darkens the hand
in a village
on the outskirts
of a vast empire
faintly remembered
where bitterness itself
was a commodity
to be bartered
as a hallowing of tears.

TENEMENT WITH FALLING WOMAN

It was not your time
yet you are gone, my child
like the morning dew,
like the evening mist.

Kakinomoto no Hitomaro,
Man'yōshū, Book 2,
Poem 217

"The departed *tama* of the dead often assumed the form of a
bird. In waving his sleeves, Hitomaro was performing a
tama-furi rite to call back his wife's spirit."

Gary L. Ebersole,
Ritual Poetry and the
Politics of Death in Early Japan

I

In those days one did not speak
of such things,
shame defined by sepia in the family album.
My mother and her sisters
had socked the family tragedy away in those pages
like children burdened with a double dare,
forced to hold their breaths
in the deep end.
Sixty years later they could barely whisper
the name of the aunt
who had leapt to her death
one August morning,
the god-awful weight of it registering
as a trembling in their voices,
leaving us to picture
a young woman giddy
with despair
edging toward the one window
without safety bars,
the sole space
that equaled emancipation
in a stuffy sixth floor walk up.

II

Each day of that hot summer
was a stockpiling of resolve,
bearing up to a mother-in-law's Sicilian curses
whispered through pursed lips,
bracing against the flare-ups of a husband's infidelity,
bold as the mistress's matches
found each Sunday morning in the pockets
of his slacks.
No one noticed the earth beginning to slip
inexorably from beneath her,
rolling out like some cheap Hollywood set.
If they noted anything,
it was the nervous titter,
the tearful apology over the glass that slipped
from her soapy hands,
the blue that enshrouded her
as she fretted over the fruit bins
on the avenue,
floppy hat pulled low to hide those twitchy eyes,
and always behind her
the three sullen children
dragging the shopping basket
over uneven sidewalks.

III

In the old country they believed that birds
carried the spirits of the dead and the squandered souls
of the lost,
so it came as no surprise
that a pigeon should have battered the kitchen window
on the morning that she jumped
or that a whirring of wings
should have preceded the moment
when two concerned brothers in shirt sleeves
called from the foyer
and received no answer,
the sandbag heavy silence they felt

as they jagged from room-to-room
scooping up children along the way
only to find a fluttering of white drapes
and a stillness
disguised as morning breeze.

ENVOY:
You will recognize her by her waist,
girlish even at age forty
as she rocks for just a moment
in indecision on the ledge,
wingless shoulders thrust back in defiance
the skin unbearably white
as the woman feigns ascent.

TO A COLLECTOR OF SEISMOGRAPHS

My hair the red
you make of it,
framed
by a window
that the war
left untouched.
Moonlight illuminates
the frieze
behind me,
a gesture that gives
credence
to what is perpendicular
in the soul
of the supreme
minimalist.

Who would dare
begrudge
the labor
of a housebound lubber?
The data
monkeyed
beyond recognition,
and the phonograph
upon which we leaned
so heavily
in the bunker,
a needling
which apparently
deserves
only part
of the credit.

II. JUST SHORT OF ALIGHTING

THE ACTUAL COST OF FORGETTING TO DANCE

That would be a younger you
at the ball
got up
as Lou Gehrig,
the world's luckiest man
slumping toward the mike,
the bat merely a prop
and the weight of full disclosure
bearing down on us
like effigies
of our former selves,
like the tango steps
we learned
and then conveniently
forgot.

Remember when we decided
that what made a bird a bird
was not the feathers
but the wings?
You would point to
a quadrille of pigeons partnered
against the autumn sky,
an illusion you wanted
me to buy into--
the false hope
of a quick cure.
Don't make me apologize for
what the curve of your neck
meant
to me in the dip,
when a Sunday
was simply a sunny day
and the waltz,
ingeniously conceived,
always brought us
back to the starting
point.

THE SLOUCH THAT CAME TO DEFINE THE BEEKEEPER

You'll recall how I learned to perform
even the smallest task
in slow motion,
how I came to hover
like a manatee
in the smoky silence of the
morning rounds,
monitoring
the decimation,
the punctilious collapse of the colony
that remains a mystery,
sweeping the cashew-shaped
corpses into neat piles,
the crunch only making it harder
to bear,
survivor guilt
reduced to the feckless beckon of clover
in a field abandoned by all save
the wind.

Beside the fire each night
silence proves the subtlest form
of impotence,
unfolding and refolding the letter
you left in the glove compartment
of my pickup after the memorial service,
your forgiveness registering
bolder than Rorschach.
But truth told
she slipped off into the river
on my watch,
while I was sorting through the flies
and tending to a stubborn
reel.
Gone in an instant,
tied to fate that
like the unraveling of the whitewater
pays us no mind.

Finding phlox where we had expected
the sweep of scotch broom,
we meet each year
in the old Masonic cemetery
beneath a copse of white oak
where pioneers
had laid out children
lost to disease and accident
in the Sunday best that had gotten them
through long rutted days
across the continental divide.
I imagine that they too
found solace where
I now find it,
in the gentle
arc of bees
among the headstones,
the acrobat's hubris
that stops just short
of alighting.

IN THE LOCAL LANGUAGE

Underwritten,
as if the instant of understanding
were preceded
by the drill bite of stillness,
a pucker of decorum
somewhere between
a gasp and transcendence.

Filtered and muted
the gut in guttural.

All I wanted was to order food
and I have ended up encumbered
with life lessons.

The sibilance of discovery,
everything balanced on the tapered back
of one slender tone.

DULY NOTED

Misery doesn't know
what it loves or doesn't,
negotiating the ache that is the mosh pit
of passion and regret

down deep.
Out in force for the protest
we mill in obstinate circles,
disoriented pilot whales hard against the shore,
awaiting direction.

The good news is
that there is no bad news

when it comes to April,
just peace signs springing up
like crocuses,
the calliope of glittery posters
and face paint,
a big tent eagerness
to live up to a rally cry
sung round robin,
as maudlin as phlox.

Protest was patented
for such a day as this,
our children's giddiness tie-dyed
into a knotty flourish
on the marble steps of the capital.

Assaulted by the enthusiasm
of the bucket brigade
we come around at last to the sanctity
of the raised fist,
stamping blistered feet in time,
marching toward a nearly wordless rendition.

GUTTA-PERCHA BLUES

Lapis lazuli rings its own bell,
an azure to write home about
extracting tang to a bluer
ingenuity,
a certainty that starts
at the base of the tongue
and sharpens in the crucible
of aftertaste.

In praise of obsolescence,
we may come to abide
anything in good time,
the stodgy pluperfect,
the smell of trees charred
to Chiclets,
the throttle
that ignited an empire
under the jungle's rusty
canopy.

Everyman's blues
thrives on persistence,
a melody line that inhabits you
before you can bear it.
When asked,
tell them it sounds better
in double time,
as if mood were merely an excuse
for the royal blue eyeliner
reserved for the boy king's
death mask.

HUNKERING

So much for the bird of paradise
surmised on the handheld
beneath the canopy's filtered light,
so much for karaoke in the underground shelter,
the stigmata of the twelve string
and the miracle of rayon,
small consolations
for those who have learned to savor the art
of settling in and waiting on
storms that never come.

We naturally took the ukulele
on the wall for a prop.
How then to explain the revelation
of the spirited accompaniment
to the Beatles' medley sung in rounds,
love me do
and battening the hatches
of our better selves,
the previous night's humidity
that clung to us
hissing out in all directions.

Swelter and wonder
in the world's quaintest
bunker,
as we pursue in earnest
the lowdown on the violin
case left on a park bench moments
before the sirens called us back to our
shadowy existence,
before I had even mentioned
hydrangeas as an option.

ILL EQUIPPED TO RESOLVE AN ECHO

Huckleberry is not a luxury
but neither is it completely
necessary.
We have allowed ourselves to be lured
off the unmarked trail
where bark dust defers to trillium,
the splay of the fork
unraveling truant,
a pittance to pay
for fealty.

The send up is always the same,
invasive species fierce against the margins
until they yield their source.
Trepidation virtually suffices
for the pilgrim
renewing desire as traction,
the rise of mist off of Onion Lake
serving to settle old scores.

Fortunately for us
Summer hardly ever dares
to hold us accountable.
Stumped by honeysuckle
we recant,
intentionality
reconfigured as the thrust
of wild ginger and fairy bells
in a grandson's fist.

ODE TO THE LEAST REMEMBERED OF JUPITER'S MOONS

The name is on the tip of my tongue,
something like justice spelled backwards,
a hectoring sibilance
that knows no quit,
the phonetic equivalent of the crazed jag
of the doctor's penlight
perturbing the ceiling of the exam room.

Let us celebrate the built-in eccentricities
of a runt moon
freakish by design,
a straying pinpoint of light
that begs restitution,
the orbit in turn mimicking
the ornate curve of the Faberge egg,
an illusion drafted in the grayest
corner of the solar system.

In junior high science club
circa 1975
things came into focus.
My father would adjust the finder
and call us up one-by-one
to gaze into the eternity of the suburban night
from the parking lot of the abandoned drive-in.
Reverently, we would squint on cue,
pretending to see what he wanted
us to see,
devising patterns,
specks to pin our hopes on.

Sonny Rollins had a name
for just such punctures of light
seen from the rail of a bridge
with the city folding behind him like wings.
I imagine the man knew something
about moons and revolutions,
about the price
we all must pay for tracking.
Hard to imagine a better form

of awe
than the altissimo
that sweetened the arc of epiphany
on a nearly moonless night.

CONSIDER IT DONE

The canyon offers alternative definitions
of home,
landscape contesting color
until the truth emerges,
a shimmer that you likely missed
as you bent to tie your laces.

In the swale between the abandoned mine
and the wide river
we made do with
the indecision of the red winged blackbird
and the pumpernickel
that we stuffed into the pockets of our overalls
out of spite.

While the elders recovered in the tents
in the wake of the feast of small deliverances,
we hunkered down in the ravine,
a tapestry of gneiss at our backs.
Fires smoldered in small pockets on the valley floor,
a fistful of stars still puncturing the horizon.

The pact was made with blood and spit,
manifest destiny wrangled
to the awakening needs
of four gangly revolutionaries.
Somehow we were going to be different,
truer to goals we could not quite grasp,
to ideals we nearly believed in.

THE SHORT VERSION

I will settle again
for the bones,
and if not the bones

then the marrow,
and if not the marrow
then the ventriloquy

of the double take,
and if not the double take
then the consolation of chrysanthemums

on a sunlit porch at dusk
saw-toothed and avuncular,
a heady reminder
of what's really at stake.

THE FINAL STAGE OF INCOGNITO

I draw the line
at the vulnerability
of orchids,
the reticence of indigo
broadcast through a scrum
of light, aloofness
trained to our expectations.
One could nearly taste
the elaboration of salt water taffy
on the boardwalk
toward dusk,
caught in summer's first real soaker.

In the thick of it
adolescence didn't look the part,
the pithy black and white of film noir
at the Rialto,
debonair in name only,
a fuzziness we could just make
out as longing.

Exasperation was merely the tip,
the desperate lunge
of late summer writ large,
chrome and pitch and cocoa butter collaborated
in the parking lot
beyond the dune grass.
In the commotion,
I conveniently forgot
to acknowledge
the patented move.

SELECTIVE MEMORIES OF THE HOEDOWN

Let us agree
to disagree about the details,
taking comfort in mesmerizing turns of phrase,
feigning outrage at the suggestion
of the dosy doe
and the temporary solace of sawdust.

Where once we stood balanced
on the margin of decorum
beleaguered by savage tautologies
we now hold our near beer aloft
in stock salute
to the caller
gaunt in machismo
sporting the muttonchops of bravado,
barking words of warning
to the lethargic.

What it meant to rise
to the occasion circa 1974,
mounting another petty campaign
to rid ourselves
of the bitterness that clings to the tongue
as doctrine,
a flame licking the certainty of knowing
exactly what the chatter of our teeth meant.

The band
prepares to rev it up again
and again
I beg to differ,
loathe to admit
that lack of syncopation
may have been our only crime.

THE DISMAL PAEAN OF ST. EL ZILCHO

"The opposite of depression is not happiness but vitality..."
Andrew Solomon, *The Noonday Demon:*
An Atlas of Depression

Catharsis
we have been taught takes
many forms: the broom handle
redesignated as a stickball bat, the teacup
poodle, polka dots and/or
the polka,
the Harley rumble for which apparently even
a patent doesn't suffice,
the sheen of the burl
and the creamy elegance of ranch.

And for that matter salve,
the diligence
with which light promotes healing
on the downward slope
without even trying,
the way toes tip naturally
toward tulips just out of reach,
everyman's *doppelgänger*
calculated
in the deep end
solely by undulation
and by a vague foreboding
about where it is that the drop off
really begins.

THE STONES' LAST GOOD ALBUM

We took what the Etruscans gave us,
shards
and rough-limbed statecraft.
Awakened too early,
we drew together artfully,
small clusters of natural allies
harboring petty grievances.

Daylight found you wanting,
huddled beside a pale fire
tawny but approachable
the hiss of the speakers
at Altamont
where light plays
around a clutch of figures swirling
in a fine rain.

It was the season of leopard skin
and tedium,
the chosen few lighting out
before our parents stumbled down
to their instant coffee,

to the rhythm of oars breaking the surface
and medicine jars with notes left in our wake.
We took the Stones and the Etruscans for granted
on those long summer nights,
and look at where it has gotten us.

THE WORD FOR THE SMELL OF TATAMI BEFORE THE PLUM RAINS

I will not fall prey
again
to the mock
sensitivity of the fern,
or be undermined
by the ice sculptor
who recasts her worst
moments
in slow motion
as slush.

For the record
that was not you
but me just beyond
the edge of the photo
skittish
in the uber gloss
of the smudged border,
unease measured
in a pitiless

dripping from the eaves,
and in the crank
of the radiator
weighing in
from the apartment
above,
opening act
for the tenor
at his daily scales

that awakened me
then you and the dog
to the whoosh
of the Magellanic Clouds,
the gabardine knot
of memory
whittled

to a nub,
as ramshackle
as a shower of blossoms.

III. WHITE KNUCKLED IN MY ADORATION

A NEW IMPROVED VERSION OF THE LIFE RAFT CONUNDRUM

This time we settle on three
sitting shoulder to shoulder,
surrounded by twelve life jackets,
a surfeit of small, friable fish
and a single hibachi.
We wait with bated breath
for pearls of wisdom
to fall from the sky

like memories of a crudely made
eclipse periscope,
a teacher's reluctant permission
to peer slantwise at a ballyhooed sun.

Back then
we had little choice
but to entrust our futures
to the limitless possibilities
of space and impressively arranged mirrors,
though the unreeling of the bungee
should have been the first sign
that things were not what they seemed.

Apropos the raft
it is worth mentioning
the single oar,
a hastily drawn sail awaiting
a stiff breeze.
The faint odor of barbecued fish
portends some development,
the inevitable emergence of alliances
and power shifts,
the gurgling that might be the springing
of a leak,
the moral dilemma reduced
to the fetish of pitch and
the roil of ambiguity.

REDBANK

Elegiac
and white knuckled in my adoration.
The shimmy of a thought
less clear caroming
toward just that spot
where the clutch of girls had been standing
only moments earlier.

But we might have been wrong
about fervor,
about the hatbox stuffed with photos
that served as a grandson's tribute.
My brother was the second
from the left, third row,
the beginning of an afro.
Semblances.

Startled but circumspect
in the shadows of the turnpike,
a sorting out of legitimate concerns
on that sunlit morning
with the big man
urging us on toward
penitence.

ANATOMY OF MY FINER MOMENTS

I love three versions of my two daughters,
each coming to me as drawings or pressed flowers
found in the pages of volumes half finished,
the bird book and the fashion show,
the startled warmth of fluorescence.

The light returns as emptiness
on my lap
where my dread lately sat.

GUFF

The other shell,
the one you dared not hold up to your ear
for fear
of what might emerge

tells a different story,
a series of epiphanies on the causeway
toward the beach where
once we stumbled upon a bone
the size of a knuckle
in the shape of a fish,
a shimmer in the memory of a boy less prodigal.

That summer,
minting what I mistook for memory
the tremble of shadow
on a summer dress,
the iridescence where I remembered it,

in the darkness
I brush away something
that may turn out to be grass
or pity.

THE SWISS CABINET MAKER
For John Fandel

That is the poet-in-residence as a boy,
his frame spare,
how prepositions like memory
understand only the physics of ambush.
On the day I turned thirty

there were signs everywhere
that I chose to ignore.
There is a word for this
in almost every language
except mine.

The wood troubled
the warp rendering them useless.
We found ourselves sorting,
looking for orthodoxy.

The artist learned to fend for himself early,
a pale boy with amazing posture.

KID YOU NOT

I had forgotten the word bleach
so settled for Clorox,
an accommodation that
kept my shirts white
while I endured yet another interrogation
in the exam room,
harboring a goat-getting pettiness,
about the very idea of memory loss.
And still I dare not doctor the inventory of dementia,
the hegemony of forgetfulness
retrofitted
to the slough of nostalgia,
fluster and regret
buffering even as I speak.

You lean in
to remind me of the pattern of stop signs
on the way to the market,
and the lacing of bougainvillea
beside the bookstore
that I had always been partial to,
chlorophyll's apathy justified
to a bum rush of memories netted
in the strewn twilight sun
following a sudden downpour,
the synapse
which translates so neatly.

When we are safely home
I may ask you to help me pen
an encomium to bony hips,
to mouth the sweet words
that always precede the inevitable bloom
of excavation,
and I will admit to you the way
that lute and loot
never so neatly fitted to the word search
give me the willies,

just as I steel myself
against the inevitable loss
of Jello's storied magenta.

OPEN MIKE NIGHT IN THE BACK ROOM OF MR. MUCK'S

The song had never really been about cars
but about a girl
left at a truck stop in the pouring rain
and about the hat
that the magician refused to surrender
to his fiercest critics
even as he willingly subjected himself
to the ignominy of dry ice.

We had long endured your defense
of Teflon and disco,
so the samovar
and the largesse of the deviled eggs
left by our door
should have come as no surprise,
paprika ground
to deliverance,
something to pin our hopes on.

By the summer of graduation,
having outlasted the CB's mindless chatter,
having negotiated
the abracadabra of the eight track,
we learned to relish the past,
swinging back naturally
to the protocol of feedback and patchouli,
discovering beneath the urgency of the strobe
reticulations to take up the slack,
too stunned to admit
that funky never tasted so good.

DEADPAN

I know what you mean
about the whiteness of paper,
the inevitability of the sharpened pencil
and the exactitude of the forgotten
line that curves
to the contours of the robin's egg
discovered beneath a hammock
resting on the freshly cut grass,
speckled for all it's worth.

You talk about the weight
we all must learn to bear,
about the nutmeg
you heard as a child
before you smelled it,

because so much is lost
in translation
at least in theory,
the way the knuckleball
flutters and resists
understanding and gravity.
The way each Thursday
figures me
in the sparse shade provided by the simile
of a date palm.

HEART MARK WHERE THE SKY WAS
9/11/2011, Edgewater, New Jersey

The care with which clouds pucker
around the wound.
I was there,
so were you
when summer seemed to lose
its bearing
and the ice on the saucer
slid in impossible angles of abandon.

That sound you can barely make out
from this distance
is the sound of practiced hands
shielding the ears of the uninitiated
from a song hung
on bones of glass.
It was not supposed to be this way,
but the winds that hug the ground
remain jaundiced and skittering.

That light you can almost discern with the naked eye
is a curio bouncing in the mirror
clutched by a baby
in the back of a plane barreling
toward anxious grandparents,
a hologram in the bluest sky
in the memory of a man
with one hand raised
pointing,
the other covering his mouth.

ONE MAN'S TRIBUTE TO ARBOREAL CREATURES

Be sure to stand with legs braced
to the pitch of the world beneath your feet.
When you finger goalpost the lens up toward your intended,
squint like John Ford at the gap in the canopy
where the rustling of branches
precedes the unspectacular flutter of premonition.

I knew a kid in high school art class
who knew that he was the spitting image
of Jim Morrison. There was a song that we all learned
on guitar but for one chord;
never quite got it.
This became
our undoing.
When you fall,
as inevitably you will,
learn to stick the landing.

What we want our children to take away from haiku,
the purchase of syllable
swaying jenga-like beneath
a corruption of sunlight
through a committed interstice of branches.

Suck it up seems to be order the day
sunlight sputtering through the green riot of eternal summer.

SUMMERSTOCK: A TRIPTYCH

The first one is insular
like a kiss during wartime,
the clemency of the fractured rib
for an aging boxer
down but not out.

Sunlight is hardship
for the sightless
in the second act.
The warmth that was the sepia
of a mother's kiss.

On three
an old man's memory
of a barbershop quartet
heard on a summer's evening
is one kind of sanctity,
these torn jeans,
the torque of the falling branch
in my hands
yet another.

YOU ARE FORGIVEN

For the incense
that clings to you like dread
and for the abstinence
that might be a foreshadowing
of flowers lost
in the half light of dusk
on a road bent on recession.

I had almost forgotten
the prognosis,
an elevation of legs
underwater,
when autumn ceased to matter
to a young man
good with machines
for whom the blues weren't nearly
what they seemed.

THE DIFFERENCE BETWEEN LACQUER AND VARNISH

It mattered to my grandfather
and his ilk,
but you would never have known
it to look at him
hunched over the wood,
mumbling Hank Williams as he scanned the planks
for warps and imperfections.

What shone in those puffy eyes
was mischief,
the tomfoolery
that kept him on a short leash
as a boy
in Hell's Kitchen,
beholden to the ice man
for the notes that he secretly passed
to a girl with pierced ears,
two blocks down
but a world away.

No time like the present
he half croons to me with a wink.
I hold the boards straight
and ice the cooler when the beer gets warm.
I keep the two soup cans marked lacquer and varnish
on opposite sides of the work bench.
Each apparently serves a purpose
though he never explains.

The brush hovers for a moment in his hand
as he searches for the ending
of verse two.
He settles on varnish,
homing in on
the right starting point,
the next best thing to harmony.

IV. MIND YOUR EUREKA

AN EVEN FINER KETTLE OF FISH

Tut ought to be remembered
for the uncommon touch,
for eccentricities that spun out like hieroglyphs
in the torchlight
and for the tattooed incisors
glowing phosphorescent for just a moment
after the mask was lifted,
a stunt
we nearly fell for
in the theme park darkness
of a museum tomb.

That was the summer that we ended
up on Dyckman Street,
up-up-upper west side,
learning to negotiate
Dylan and
the woman upstairs who blackened
her teeth
as a matter of course.
She would turn aside
in the stairwell
when we met
to make room for what was left
of the moonlight,
as if she had an inkling
about grace,
a premonition as sensible
as the gizzard.

We had come too late to graffiti,
long after the canonization
of Basquiat and Haring,
long after Steve Martin
had already taught us everything
that we needed to know
about the boy king
and his sacred habits.

SNAKE OIL

Defined not for the first time by the quest
for cough medicine,
extracting the inner peddler,
a bunching
in the slack angles of the *hutong,*
another vain attempt to revert
to the huckster the old man
hoped to make of me.

The efficacies spill out
in lazy ropes,
coagulations of memory,
the bittersweet of butterscotch netted
like the coelacanth
on a lazy Beijing summer afternoon.

The shimmer of *Astrophel and Stella*
rediscovered in a college textbook
caught me and later you
by surprise
and quickly proved a burden
beside the lake
at the Summer Palace,
salve to the wound on the hand
that spins the prayer wheel.

The anatomically correct equation
is a scrawl within the darkened outline
of the space where Mao's poster
used to hang.
Hand me a wrench so that I can undo
the longing for a father
long overdue
that you and I might again be drawn as
scar-crossed lovers
through a labyrinth
more imagined than real.

EARTH CALLING DICKEY BETTS

From the beginning
the magnolias mattered too much,
so I swept them
into my best shot at disarray.
Lost again on Jupiter Boulevard,
sticking the chords I fretted

in my wayward youth,
I earned amicable
but bartered for a better
version of myself.
The ayes have it,
erstwhile chops and licks
silhouetted on the rocks or neat,
juking for juking's sake
linoleum smooth
what began as bass—
just shy of delectable.

Donning the imperial yellow,
the king of the bent note fiddles
with his fuzz box,
though truth to be told
from the nosebleeds everyone looks
smaller than life.

HAVING FAILED TO MEMORIZE EVEN THE MISSION STATEMENT

When the time comes,
we may choose to remember the way
rain clung to pine that morning
like a drunken lover's
apology.

MY OWN BEESWAX

It's funny you should mention
eucalyptus,
the last whiff of causation
cruising D Street which crosses D River
described until recently
as the world's shortest.
It was precisely at that juncture
that we ran smack dab
into the secessionists' idea
of a block party,
the choral comeuppance
of a barbershop quartet
weighing in
on the gamble we wagered,
eloquence
as simple a thing as my fist unbudding
after the rare double pump.
Hunky dory in the moonlight,
the inspiration that started as macadam
ended unceremoniously
at the door of the former
Anarchist, another slacker
who didn't look the part.

NEARLY THE COMPLETE OPPOSITE OF CHECKMATE

Supposing there are times when a rainy day
is remembered precisely as a rainy day,
the droop of the quintessential lilac just beyond the fence
tidy as the scrimshaw shaking
in a great-uncle's upturned hands.

We arrived at the shared summer cottage just after you,
precocity only making my stutter worse.
I'm almost certain that I read somewhere
something to the effect that
at age fifteen no one should be held accountable
for the alchemy
that makes gibberish of desire.

In the afterglow
of a late summer evening
the graininess of mutual indifference
flushed the corners of the room that the light
failed to fathom,
a host of board games
to tide us.
Secured by the magnificent force of afterthought,

I made a move
akin to the elbowy architecture
of a child's chalk rainbow.

On our last night on the island
you hesitated beneath the neon
of Dave's Cafe
and dared to whisper what we both had known
all along:
the Mohawk had arrived too late
to do me any good.

THE FINE ART OF SHENANIGANS

Unencumbered
The keen ascends,
fattening to hullaballoo.
Under the refuge of a shawl
an old woman rocks
akimbo in her grief,
banshee teeth crooked
in something like a grin.

In my folding chair
at the back of the waking room
I finger a photo
of me as a boy
crowded by a man
they wanted me to call
Uncle Squid,
a man who arrived in front of the house
like clockwork in a truck
once every three years.

Himself laid out
in all his glory,
a life lived beneath
the brim of a tweed cap
under faded eaves,
Inwood and Washington Heights,
the copper of blood on his lips
after another scuffle with the cops
on a block where
everyone was an enemy.

In the absence
of a father,
it was his job
to give me the belt,
beating three years' worth of a boy's mischief
out of me.
I would relish the game,
the zig and zag
from room to room,

his heart not in it,
a tired shaking of the head,
fulfilling righteous duties.

Later there would be ice cream
and apologies in the shape of mumbles,
a conspiracy of winks
across the table,
letting the drinks fizz
to mask our relief.

Grant me this one absolution,
a backward glance
to an old woman left wheezing
in the corner and beyond
to you in front of the Parkgate Tavern,
Your right hand raising a Rheingold in mock salute,
the left upturned as supplicant,
gap-toothed Maitreya,
the hint of a rakish grin
from under the shadow of your visor.
Always the last laugh.

HARD BOP 101

I learned the rudiments of sailing
as a child from an old jazzman,
the chop and noodle of tide
reconfigured as hands freckled to the wheel.

Alone on the deck pining to escalate,
to strut like Dizzy hailing a cab
on nights when the smell of turpentine
clung to the evening air like the fragments of a riff.

Half convinced to concede to sun and brine,
I awaken to a pulsing that begins
as amnesia and flourishes as foreshadow
of an acolyte's stab at moonlight and mist.

Lovers construe the bass line literally
as a diphthong of passion discovered in lower registers,
the way a clutch of gulls is wholly absolved
by the horizon: the messenger in every sailor's son.

THE SECRET LIVES OF PUNCTUATION

If you expect a great deal
from the comma
you will always be disappointed,
as with the spleen

the way it sulks
in an indeterminate spot
within the fold of the guts,
doing god knows what,

a paradox wrapped inside an enigma
hard against a semicolon.
So too the rent-a-cop insouciance
of parentheses,

the careful but not cautious
mediation of the ellipsis,
a drop off that mimics
the folding of the unknown soldier's flag

on a misty August morning,
the dash's incredulity aping
the kid brother who never knows
when to keep his big trap shut.

The windmill in every air
guitarist's arsenal prompts
the whoosh of the apostrophe
as it finds purchase,

the big top optimism of italics
announcing nothing to it, really,
just another tree
for the barking,

and if in the end we say period
we mean period, essentially
the buck stops here

.

NOTES FROM AN UNREDEEMED SON

Sunlight seen through veins
is a comfort,
empathy emerging as shadow from the IV bag,
the second son's
filial piety defined
by a Tuesday afternoon's
promise of rain.

Noticeably thinner
in corduroy,
your thumb poised to smudge
a lifetime of indecision
in the turkey grease
on the tray table.
What lately I mistook for coursing
is in fact
a litany of contamination.

You were not meant to die in spring—
This much we know,
lessons learned on a road trip
to Baja,
a fortuneteller in an ill-fitting turban,
how your fingers seek to remember
the contours of old photos
while I massage your feet.
In search of loopholes,
I resort to the rite of the double take,
waiting on
an intercession of sorts.

WHY MAYBELLENE

A weekend squandered in the library,
your quest to pin down the Sanskrit for hayride
finds me bucking trends,
conceding the long-awaited ski trip to the Poconos.

Not to be outdone,
I linger over Divisadero,
scuttle to commit to memory
the entry after Gulag.

As good as lost,
the afternoon tracks snow as clean as afterthought,
hot cocoa and the hearth
that might have been.

Left to my devices
I dredge up memories of a spelling bee
gone horribly wrong,
the verb that rhymed with slake,
the stutter that
still troubles
recitation,
the sole inheritance
from a word-obsessed father.

Getting warmer,
you size up the seven words for slush in Inuit,
just as we lose our passion for the hunt,
and head out
to a parking lot rendered silver by
an unattended moon.

Magic sic madrigal
ala Chuck,
the understated question:
why can't you be true?

PULLING IVY

Having become a believer
in the value of native species,
I give over my Saturday
to pulling invasives
in the state park near my home.

I recognize inertia
when I feel it,
having relearned the art of tugging
rather than yanking.

Elysium and all that is misconstrued
in a morning's dapple,
the bind of ivy in a bend in the creek
apes my recovery,
a small price to pay.

Rootedness is no small thing
to the native,
however defined.

RELATIVE TRUTHS ABOUT THE OBJECTS OF MY AFFECTION

Don't by fooled by the cicadas' practiced indifference
or the surly chatter of moss being moss.
Only recently have we come to abide
the price paid
for the false piety of summer,
the green-gray smithereens
of algae and frogs' eggs
prismatic
in the puddle beside the mailbox,
an issue that never gets any smaller.

THE BURDEN OF THE DOUBLE YOLK

You assure me that it is not really a time of war
and that I will notice the difference immediately.
How can I then not fail to be comforted

by the silence of the fruit vendors as they weave
in and out among the abandoned pickup trucks,
or by the laughter of children who trade batteries for flowers

in the shade of the peace wall and who recoil
at the bleating of goats on the way to the abattoir?
The table clothes at the expat cafe are bleached

beyond anything that might be construed as white
and diners learn to ignore the double yolk at their own risk,
healthy superstitions reduced to the dates spoiling

on the windowsill, while we argue with the village
headman yet again about the world's fourth oldest profession—
learning to lean on God in the absence of the abacus.

In the cool of the evening I remember my sister's
hands, artisanal and gaunt as they measured flour
with practiced elegance beneath a yellowed paper lamp

the night before the sabbath. Every shadow that fell across our feet
that morning protested the chastity of parchment,
a betrayal of the ghost that wasn't quite a ghost.

Even before the blast we knew that it would be big
and would only get bigger in the way of revelations.
Precious, you ask? It all depends on what you mean by precious.

ACKNOWLEDGMENTS

The author wishes to thank the editors at the following publications where the poems listed below originally appeared, sometimes in slightly altered form:

Big River Poetry Review: "Hard Bop 101"
Borderlands: Texas Poetry Review: "The Slouch that Came to Define the Beekeeper"
Burningword Literary Journal: "Ballad for One Who Tenders the Bas-Relief," "Deadpan," "That Which the Water Embraces"
Clackamas Literary Review: "Heart Mark Where the Sky Was"
Columbia Review: "Relative Truths About the Objects of My Affection"
Faultline: "Tenement with Falling Woman"
Lindenwood Review: "I Stand Corrected"
Minetta Review: "In the Attic of Small Remembrances"
Muddy River Poetry Review: "The Swiss Cabinet Maker"
Poetry Quarterly: "Consider It Done"
Spoon River Poetry Review: "Secret Handshake of the Minor Bachs"
Straylight Literary Magazine: "In the Local Language," "Notes of an Unredeemed Son," "One Man's Tribute to Arboreal Creatures," "You'll Remember Matilda,"
Stolen Island: "Snake Oil"
Syndic Literary Journal: "The Fine Art of Shenanigans," "Summerstock," "You Are Forgiven"
Tule Review: "Redbank"
Wilderness House Literary Review: "The Final Stage of Incognito"

ABOUT THE AUTHOR

Christopher T. Keaveney received his undergraduate degree in English from Manhattan College and his MA in Japanese Language and Literature and Ph.D. in Comparative Literature from Washington University in St. Louis. He also pursued graduate studies at Tsukuba University in Ibaraki, Japan and at Fudan University in Shanghai and taught abroad in American Samoa, Japan, and China. Keaveney currently teaches Japanese language and East Asian literature and film courses at Linfield College in McMinnville, Oregon and is the author of three books about Japanese culture and Sino-Japanese literary relations. His poetry has appeared in *Columbia Review, Spoon River Poetry Review, Borderlands: Texas Poetry Review, The Minetta Review, Stolen Island, Faultline, Wilderness House Literary Review*, and elsewhere, and several of his English language haiku have appeared in the *Mainichi Daily News*. He lives in Portland with his wife Shigeko and his daughters Bridget and Erica.